KITTEN TO TIGER

ANIMALS GROWING UP

Jason Cooper

ROURKE CLASSROOM RESOURCES
The path to student success

Vero Beach, Florida 32964

www.rourkepublishing.com

PHOTO CREDITS: All photos © Lynn M. Stone except p. 4 © Keren Su

Title page: *While her kittens play, a tiger cools off in the water.*

Editor: Frank Sloan

Cover design by Nicola Stratford

Library of Congress Cataloging-in-Publication Data

Cooper, Jason, 1942-
  Kitten to tiger / by Jason Cooper.
      v. cm. — (Animals growing up)
Includes bibliographical references (p.   ).
Contents: Tigers — Newborn tigers — Tiger kittens growing up.
  ISBN 1-58952-695-3 (hardcover)
  1. Tigers—Infancy—Juvenile literature. [1. Tigers. 2. Animals—Infancy.] I. Title. II. Series: Cooper, Jason, 1942-
Animals growing up.

  QL737.C23C67458 2003
  599.756—dc21

                                              2003007272

Ppk 1-58952-858-1

Printed in the USA

CG/CG

Table of Contents

Tigers

The biggest tigers are the largest of cats. Some male tigers weigh about 600 pounds (273 kilograms). They have tremendous strength and quickness to go with their long, sharp teeth and claws.

Tigers are **predators**, or meat-eaters. They kill other animals, their **prey**, for food. Tigers can kill hoofed animals larger than themselves. A wild tiger may gobble down 90 pounds (41 kilograms) of meat in one sitting!

A tiger usually kills prey with a powerful bite to the throat.

Wild tigers live only in Asia. And they live in some pretty amazing places, from fearsome cold to extreme heat. A tiger's dense fur helps keep it warm in cold places, like Russia. Tigers in tropical rain forests and hot grasslands have to stay cool! They do so by swimming.

A tiger may grow up in a cold forest or in a hot jungle or grassland.

Newborn Tigers

Tiger kittens may be born at any time, but most often they're born in the spring or summer. They're 3-pound (1.3-kilogram) fur balls with eyes shut. **Instinctively**, however, they find their mother's milk. A tiger usually has two to four kittens, but she may have as many as seven.

The mother **nurses** the kittens. She hides them from predators such as leopards, wolves, bears, and big male tigers. If she senses danger, she carries each kitten in her mouth to a new hideout.

A mother tiger is everything to her kittens, even a pillow!

Before it is two weeks old, a tiger kitten opens its eyes. For several weeks it lives on its mother's milk and the prey the mother brings back. Meanwhile, the kittens play-fight with each other. That helps sharpen their instincts to **stalk**, charge, and attack.

Kittens prepare for life as predators with playful battles.

Tigers grow quickly. At five or six months of age the kittens begin following their mother to kills. And in the next few months, they follow her as she hunts. By watching mom, the youngsters learn how and what to kill. And they learn from a master hunter.

Adult male tigers generally live alone, except when **courting** a female. A father tiger has no role in raising his youngsters.

A young tiger, less than a year old, pads after its mother.

Tiger Kittens Growing Up

Tiger kittens can often make their own kills just before they're a year old. They are not fully grown, but they are already big cats. Some of them weigh more than 300 pounds (136 kilograms).

Within the next six months, young tigers get permanent adult teeth. They have more killing power and a new sense of **independence**.

This tiger is still just 15 months old and not yet independent.

Between the age of 18 months and two years, young tigers leave their mother. It isn't always their choice. But the mother now has a new litter of kittens. She chases her older kittens away. Young females may stay in their mother's home neighborhood for a while. Males, however, tend to wander away, looking for their own territories.

For a while at least, this young female will probably stay in her mother's home area.

This is a very dangerous time for young male tigers. They may enter territories of older, stronger males. When fights follow, the young tigers are often killed or badly injured. They may also wander into villages and be shot. So, despite having a tiger for a mom, a kitten has a tough time growing up.

Male tiger fights can result in serious injury, usually for the younger tiger.

19

In any tiger litter, only one or two is likely to survive its first two years. Some are born too weak to survive. Others die from disease or from predators. And many young males die fighting or from their wounds.

Tigers that do grow up are truly the kings of the jungles, grasslands, and forests. Some have lived to the age of 26.

But tigers in the wild are in danger of dying out. In fact, there may be as few as 4,000 wild tigers.

Speed, power, and keen senses make tigers near-perfect predators.

A tiger kitten begins to hunt early in life.

Glossary

courting (CORT ing) — the behavior used to win a mate

independence (in dee PEN dents) — acting by oneself without the help of others

instinctively (in STINGK tiv lee) — acting with the behaviors with which an animal is born, rather than acting with learned behaviors

nurses (NURSS ez) — giving a mother's milk to offspring, or for offspring to take mother's milk

predators (PRED uht urz) — animals that hunt other animals for food

prey (PRAY) — an animal that is hunted by another animal for food

stalk (STOCK) — to hunt by moving forward slowly and quietly toward a victim

Index

Further Reading

Markert, Jenny. *Tigers*. Child's World, 1998
St. Pierre, Stephanie. *Siberian Tigers*. Heinemann Library, 2001
Weisbacher, Ann. *Tigers*. Abdo, 2000

Websites To Visit

www.5tigers.org/Directory/kids.htm
www.seaworld.org/infobooks/Tiger/home.html

About The Author

Jason Cooper has written several children's books about a variety of topics for
Rourke Publishing, including the recent series *Eye to Eye With Big Cats* and *Holiday
Celebrations*. Cooper travels widely to gather information for his books. Two of his
favorite travel destinations are Alaska and the Far East.